"I'm very impressed with this book's down-to-earth, practical and user-friendly advice. It will be very accessible to a wide range of parents and it never talks down to them. Plus, the 'Don't' and 'Do' illustrations are fun! I will recommend it to parents in my practice who could use the help."

- Cerise Morris M.S.W., Ph.D.

"Practical advice in language everyone can understand."

- Nicolette De Smit M.S.W.

How to be an (Almost) Perfect Parent

Dos and Don'ts from a former
Family Support Worker

Ellie Presner

ISBN 978-0-9695957-7-9
How to be an (Almost) Perfect Parent
Dos and Don'ts from a former
Family Support Worker

All identifying details have been changed, including names, except for the author's own children. Some of the material in this book appeared in the author's booklets published in 1989 and 1990. This book is not intended as a substitute for advice from a licensed professional.

Cover photo: Painting of Elisa Bonaparte with her daughter Napoleona Baciocchi, by François Gérard (1770-1837) – Wikimedia Common

Table of Contents

Having children makes you no more a parent than having a piano makes you a pianist.

- Michael Levine

~~~

For my perfect November babies, Kathryn, 1968

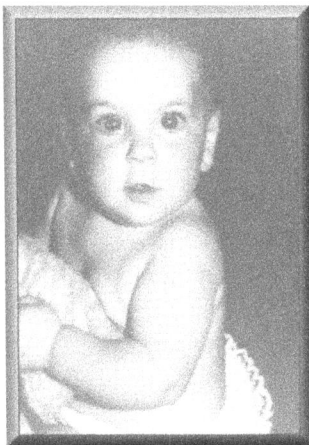

...and Jeremy, 1972

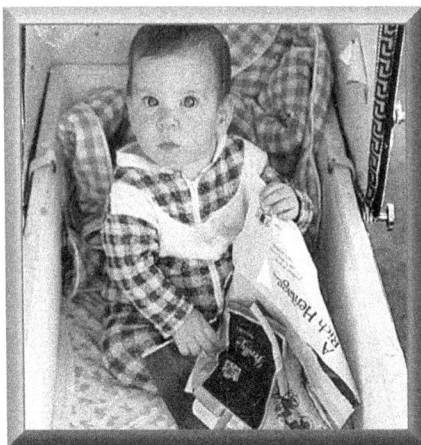

1. Why I wrote this book

Okay, so did you notice the epigraph on a previous page by one "Michael Levine"? No, I don't know who he is either, but he sure came up with a great line! There are a few ways we can learn how to be good parents:

- We can, for example, be lucky enough to have them ourselves, and then when it's our turn, try to emulate them.

- Another way is if we have lousy parents, we can try to do the *opposite* to what they did.

- Still another way is to *read* about examples of good parents and try to do what they say.

- And *another* really good way is to be shown by a parenting-skills educator in a face-to-face encounter, that there are possibly better ways to handle our kids in certain situations.

You know when you see someone doing something wrong? Maybe she's gripping a golf club incorrectly. Or he's putting a page face-up instead of face-down on the scanner. Or she changes lanes but doesn't signal with her flasher.

Clearly there's a hierarchy of "wrongs." The golf club example isn't dire, but the omission of a lane-change signal could be dicey.

I saw a similar range of parent-child interactions when I was a family support worker teaching people how to become better parents. The Dos and Don'ts I offer throughout this book are drawn from my weekly home visits with them, and I'd like to share them with you.

2. From one extreme to the other

I worked for seven years with families my supervisor would assign to me.

At one agency, I was sent to support troubled families by the Director of Youth Protection services. The family had to sign an agreement with a DYP worker to allow me to visit and help them with their kids. The goal was to improve their parenting abilities and avoid foster-home placement if at all possible.

At a different organization, the other counsellors and I responded to calls from the parents themselves. In some ways, this was harder! With the really troubled families, it was easy to see what some of the problems were, and we workers would try to help accordingly (which was *not* easy); but in the higher-functioning households, well, sometimes the parents helped *me*. I remember one mother sharing some of her cache of booklets and lists of resources with me. I shared some of ours with her too, so we had a nice exchange thing going.

We have many jobs as parents: to nurture, teach, keep safe; but – well, you know what they say about doctors: "First of all, do no harm"? My version of that for parents is the same, with the following examples.

3. First of all, DON'T be guilty of…

- Ignoring wet diapers until severe diaper rash results
- Punishing your kid by making him kneel for a while… on the floor… on uncooked rice
- Losing sight of your toddler so she wanders outside, picks up discarded food from the gutter and munches on it
- Letting your boyfriend terrify your sons at dinner with his military-like demands
- Padlocking your pantry and fridge so your starving kids can't grab something – anything!
- Sleeping in while your hungry preschoolers manage to toast a whole loaf of bread slice by slice in the toaster
- Not noticing while your little one drinks some toxic chemical from under the sink. She lives, but a stubborn casework manager ignores your endangered children, saying "foster care is just as bad; *I* was a foster child and I know."

Feel better already, you average mums and dads? Those were some of the worst situations I came across in my work with "protection"-mandated families. It was tough to see these things, as you might imagine.

I know that this book alone won't help in such extreme cases of neglect and abuse. Much more intervention is needed in such households.

But when I ended my years in the field of family support, I compiled some tips for ordinary parents coping with challenging little everyday occurrences. I gathered the tips into booklets, and sold several thousand by mail-order across the country. Many were acquired by schools, day-care centres and hospitals as well as by individual parents.

I'm expanding upon their content in this current book, in the hope that something will strike a chord with you. (I pray you'll give my less-than perfect artistic skills a pass!)

Without further ado, here are my Dos and Don'ts for parents, starting with preschoolers and working my way up to teens.

4. Dos & Don'ts – little kids, bigger kids & parents

DON'T:

> Beth, get down from the stool.
> Why?
> Because you might fall.
> I won't fall.
> I said get down!
> Don' wanna!
> Beth...

DO:

> Beth, you didn't get down from the stool like I asked you, so I will help you. The stool is only for grown-ups to climb on.
> Oh well... I tried.

Actions speak louder than words. The child feels secure; Mom shows she means what she says.

How many times do we see a parent getting into a discussion with their small offspring? Some times it's appropriate – other times it's not, as in this example.

Potentially dangerous situations are *not* negotiable.

Notice that the mom in the DO pic doesn't get angry at Beth. She simply narrates what she's doing very matter-of-factly while giving her the reason, and at the same time removing her from the danger.

Mom (or Dad, if he was here instead) is more likely to lose her cool in the DON'T pic, because she's getting into an argument with Beth, back and forth, in an endless loop. Does this sound familiar to you? Probably. I'll bet we've all done it! The thing we quickly discover is that kids can outlast us in the arguing department. I think they should all get into law school by default; they'd be great in a courtroom! They'd probably even wear down the judge!

However, that's not what we're aiming for. As parents we have the final word. *This is what we're doing,* and as they say in French, *point finale.*

Now, this is what happens in situations of danger. There are other scenarios where there can be a *bit* of discussion, as we'll soon see.

DON'T:

DO:

Sometimes it's wise to let natural consequences happen. Child feels pride in learning on her own, and an unnecessary power struggle has been avoided.

In situations like this, a good dollop of will power is called for! We parents are pretty smart, and we know that as sure as B follows A, little Janie's hands are soon going to be freezing and wet. Therefore the preventive "medicine" is for Janie to wear her "waterpoof" mittens.

However, headstrong Janie has other ideas. She wants to wear the purple wool ones she got for _____ (fill in with her birthday, Christmas, or just a little gift from her favourite auntie…). But: Wool. Isn't. Water-proof.

So how about this: let her wear them. What's the worst that could happen? Her hands get real cold, real wet, real fast.

Great! Janie will have just learned a valuable lesson in consequences, *all by herself!* She will learn something and get a self-esteem boost at the same time.

You had that hand towel ready for her, right, Mom? Stop that grinning!

DON'T:

DO:

Give choices often… as long as the choice that's made doesn't matter to you. Child feels proud and grown-up to have some control over events.

Giving choices to little ones is a fabulous way to manage behaviour that could otherwise be troublesome. The key thing to remember is this: *Whichever way the child decides, it shouldn't matter to you!* So we must only use this tactic when the choice isn't important to us.

The fallout from doing this is clearly a win-win. The child makes the choice for us. How great is that? *And* the child is in control – for once in his/her little life. Can you imagine how good that makes him feel?

There are so many occasions when we can use the strategy of giving choices:

● Getting dressed – do you want the blue socks or the brown ones?

● Parts of a meal – do you want the bagel or the roll? Do you want the carrots or the sweet potato?

● Sleep toys – do you want to sleep with Dotty Doll or Dippy Dawg?

You get the idea. Each time we let our children make a choice like this, we're giving them agency, control, that they don't otherwise often have. It boosts their self-esteem. More on self-esteem to come.

DON'T:

DO:

It's better to give advance notice to help smooth transition times. Child feels respected: her activities are not so trivial that they must be abruptly stopped.

Never knock the use of a timer. Why is it great? Because a child can't argue with a timer when it goes BZZZZZT!

It's a neutral object, see? Notice how the mom doesn't let on to the fact that *she's* the one who set it. (Now this works with little ones; it's true of course that older kids will catch on. See next page for another twist on this trick.)

In the DON'T panel, we can easily empathize with the child who's being told very abruptly to switch gears. Well, most of us can empathize. Right??

The DO panel oozes reason and calm. We are showing her respect, which 1) models for her how to do it; and therefore 2) will in turn come back to you tenfold one day. Respect begets respect. You'll see!

DON'T:

DO:

Letting your child save face can cut short many power struggles. Child feels parent is being reasonable. From this model she in turn can learn to make reasonable compromises.

This situation is almost identical to the previous one, with one change. Instead of a timer, the dad allots the time extension himself. This is handy when we want to be seen as the "benevolent" parent.

It's an alternative to the neutral timer. Perhaps if we don't happen to have a timer handy, we could try this. The effect is the same.

It works best if we first say they have to stop doing their activity, and upon their protest, we ever-so-kindly give them a bit more time.

Wow, are we a great parent! We have just magically transformed from a demanding, cruel ogre to a kindly, old… nice guy.

DON'T:

DO:

Channel your child's energy to prevent or stop misbehaviour due to boredom. Choices help.

Notice in the DO panel that Dad isn't coming across as acrimonious, angry, or confronting. On the contrary, he's calmly stating why John's behaviour is problematic, and then helps him by redirecting his attention. This is a valuable *distraction*.

John actually ends up feeling grateful for his parent's positive involvement. He sees that Dad cares enough to make the effort to suggest other activities – some of which his father might even share with him!

Also, *choices* again. We should always try to remember that giving kids choices is a *very* effective way to give them a little power.

However, sometimes we need to set limits more forcefully, as you'll see…

DON'T:

DO:

Set limits and stick to them. Consistency prevents chaos. The child will feel secure knowing that you mean what you say, and that the same result always occurs in such a situation.

Little kiddies are a lot like little kitties. I say that because both types of cuties thrive on consistency.

Also, I can say that because I have had both, so I know.

It's true that my illustrations oversimplify this point. In real life, it may take a few – or many – repeated instances in which you "say what you mean and mean what you say." In that case the thought balloon in the bottom picture would be amended to read: "Hmm, he said the same thing every day for the past week... I guess I'll just have to wait 'til supper."

Of course, real life (once again rearing its ugly head) can intervene and prevent us from being consistent. In that case we can try to explain as best we can why things were different *just this one time*. For example, "Yes, yesterday you had a cookie before supper because we were at Aunt Millie's house and she gave you one... because *she didn't know our rule.*" (Darn that Aunt Millie!)

Consistency is an effective goal to strive for.

DON'T:

> I told you to share your toys with Peter! Since you're not, you can't have any dessert tonight at supper!

> Aw—not fair!

DO:

> I told you to share toys. Since you're not, we won't be able to invite Peter here next time you want him to come.

> Hm-m... guess I'll have to learn to share pretty soon.

"Logical" consequences can be calmly enforced, and seem fair to the child. She senses the justice in it. The logical connection between the infraction and the result helps her to learn the desired behaviour much faster.

I want to insert a few points here about discipline. How can we teach our kids what we won't tolerate?

Let's rule out corporal punishment first. It has been shown that physical punishment as a form of discipline does not work. Why not? Because:

- We're teaching the child that "might makes right." We're bigger and stronger, so what we say goes, and usually hurts!

- The angrier we get, we can only hit harder. Is that what we want to do? Is that what we want to teach our child? How hard will we hit, how much will we hurt her/him, before we think it's enough? And how will our child feel afterward? Which leads into…

- Kids who've been punished this way tend to forget what their crime was. But they sure remember the punishment. It teaches them to be afraid of the punisher. It teaches them to try very hard in future to be cagey and sly, and try to sneak behind the punisher's back all the time. It teaches avoidance behaviour… avoidance of the parents, the very people who are supposed to be helping them to learn right from wrong.

So, no. Some ways to teach desirable behaviour are to:

- model it.
- use natural or logical consequences for bad behaviour.
- use positive reinforcement (encouragement, praise, recognition, rewards.)

Most of these strategies are illustrated in this book.

DON'T:

I told you to stop teasing Cory! Do you want a spanking!?

Wa-a! No!)

DO:

You are still teasing Cory after I told you to stop. You will have to sit in this corner for ten minutes so that you will be calmer afterward.

Aw...*

*face-saving protest; best to ignore.

Use "Time-Out" – a brief think-it-over time to counteract repeated boisterous behaviours. The child will soon feel calmer. The Time-Out breaks the escalating cycle of misbehaviour. (Attention is withdrawn, so the misbehaviour no longer pays off.)

I know that the concept of Time-Out is a bit controversial. I will say this, based on my experience with the families I visited: it usually works. Even if the Time-Out is only two minutes – and I know that two minutes can seem like twenty to a little kid who has been removed from the place "where the action is" – it's effective.

Try it firmly but without anger. You might need to practice it a few times. But you can manage it. (If I could, anyone can!)

Some people swear by making the number of Time-Out minutes equal to the number of years of the child's age. Whatever you feel is right.

Still other parents like to put *themselves* in a Time-Out. I don't recommend this if your children are very young! However, it can work wonders with older kids if Mom goes to lie down for ten minutes while they do some homework, or watch a (good, educational!) TV program, or try a jigsaw puzzle, or the like.

Our goal is to break up and redirect the children's negative behaviour.

DON'T:

DO:

Separate all who are involved in a conflict. Children will feel secure: the adult is helping them to regain control. Also, justice is served, as no one child receives all the blame.

When we have the time (and energy!), it helps to *listen* to the combatants first, before taking any action. It might become clear right away what the problem is, e.g.:

"What's the matter?"

"Jamie flushed my paper airplane down the toilet."

Okay, that's clear. But when it's not, the separation of kids works well.

If they share a room, what then? We can put them in separate corners of the same room, if possible. If it's the room *we* are in, so much the better – we can keep an eye on them and watch for any taunting.

Or we can put one child in one room and one in another. (I have to assume you live in more than a one-room hut.)

Don't forget: the calmer we are, they calmer they will be.

DON'T:

DO:

Acknowledge your child's feelings, especially anger, disappointment or sadness. The child feels that at least the parent understands; she doesn't have to continue protesting, as her feelings were acknowledged.

When our children are upset, acknowledgement of their hurt goes a long way towards making them feel better. I think we can all relate to that; I *know* I can.

Here's a childhood memory of my own. When I was little I had some food quirks (okay, I still have some). One of them was a preference for dry cereal without any milk added to it; another was a dislike for the crusts of my toast. My dad, however, had very strong ideas of how we were supposed to eat; my own likes/dislikes didn't count. I remember being made to sit at the table, and being told that I couldn't leave until I ate the way he believed I should. In the end, in tears by now, I'd be rescued by the clock: either I had to get dressed for school, or he had to leave for work – or both.

Even years later, during a Saturday lunch with my mother, she'd usually offer me tomato juice, forgetting that I had always refused it. When I'd say, "No thanks, you know I don't like it," she'd say, "Oh! But *we love* tomato juice!" The implication was that there must be *something wrong with me* because *they loved* it.

Note the DO panel opposite. How much better – better understood, more cared for – the child feels! And this understanding allows her to move on.

(P.S. – I still don't like tomato juice.)

DON'T:

DO:

Minimize negatives; focus on positives. Child feels appreciated – a very warm feeling. Self-esteem grows.

We can never give our kids too much positive attention. Notice the difference between the DON'T and DO panels. The words we say carry a ton of weight.

Here are a few more suggestions for showing positive attention:

- Give *at least* 15 minutes a day of pure "pleasant time" to each child – a worthwhile "investment"!

- Reward good behaviour and it will be repeated: hugs and kisses are free; so is saying "I love you"!

- Rewards can sometimes be tangible, such as stickers on a chart, or even a small toy. (The latter should be very seldom, though. We don't want to make them behave only for tangible payoffs.)

- Avoid comparing your kids with each other. Each one is unique; praise that uniqueness.

- Avoid negative labelling. Children tend to live up (down!) to labels. (e.g. "lazy," "clumsy")

- Treat your child the way YOU would like to be treated – with respect.

If the child doesn't get positive recognition, what incentive does he have to behave well? He'll act out just to receive *any* attention: any – to him – is better than none at all.

More on this to come…

DON'T:

Ian's my favourite, he's so good. Gary never listens to me, and Melissa always has her head in the clouds.

I'm the best!

DO:

Ian plays soccer well; Gary's a good artist, and Melissa loves her drama class.

She thinks we're all good at something!

Recognize that all your children have strengths; don't show favouritism. They'll all have higher self-esteem.

Aside from the fact that I learned how to be a bit fancier with the cartoon depictions from this point on, what are your thoughts on this?

Every child has something positive about him or her, either a trait or skill, which can be praised. A constantly overshadowed sibling may have trouble developing self-confidence. So try not to single out one of your children at the expense of the other(s).

DON'T:

DO:

Allow your kids to enjoy their own likes and dislikes. They're not copies of you. Allow their growth.

Please overlook the outdated depiction of a boom box. Today's kids would use an iPod or clone thereof, and ear buds. But the message still rings true!

The point is: we don't have to love it (their music, clothes, hairstyle, etc.) but we don't have to insult it, either. It's normal and necessary for growing children to develop tastes that differ from those of their parents. Give them some room for this growth.

The only exceptions should fall in the areas of:

- SAFETY
- HEALTH
- WELFARE

…when we *must* intervene.

And when we *do* intervene, we have to try to do it without attacking their self-esteem.

DON'T:

DO:

Share fun times whenever possible.

When was the last time your gang played together? Family activities that all enjoy should be scheduled as often as possible.

They don't have to cost money! Family play is just as important as family "work." (Of course, our teens will probably prefer the company of their peers, which is perfectly normal.)

Sharing fun will:
- lead to a new appreciation of one another
- balance the "bad" times
- alleviate guilt when we're *really* too busy.

DON'T:

DO:

Say "yes" more often than an automatic "no."

With a little creativity, we can cut the number of "no's" down by half! Family life will be more pleasant.

Let's face it, there are so many situations where parents *have* to say "no." Such times would include areas of safety, health and welfare, as mentioned earlier.

But there are times when a "no" can become a "yes." For the person on the receiving end (usually the child), it's far more tolerable to hear ten "no's" a day than, say, twenty.

DON'T:

DO:

Give them "goodies": be generous with encouragement, compliments and affection.

Parents: don't forget to give *each other* goodies! The receiver will feel terrific. The giver will feel pretty great too!

We all want recognition. We all want to feel that we're *visible,* that we *count.* The worst thing parents can do is ignore their children.

The child who is continually ignored or deprived of affection is very likely to develop behaviour problems, for she or he will try ever harder to get attention in any way possible, as alluded to earlier.

DON'T:

DO:

Single parents: give extra attention and reassurance to your kids – they need it now more than ever.

When we're just super busy, or during the emotional upheaval of marital difficulties or separation, it's easy for our children's needs to be overlooked. This is especially true of youngsters who are quiet and withdrawn, as opposed to boisterous and obviously upset.

Either type of behaviour is a signal that they are in dire need of our loving reassurance and positive attention. Our kids will feel more secure and lovable.

DON'T:

DO:

Give yourself a break: you have needs too! Occasional respite breaks are refreshing for everyone!

Regular mini-vacations are a must. Even a couple of hours off from the daily grind can help restore our energy and perspective.

This is perhaps especially true with single families, where the custodial parent has to shoulder both mom and dad roles on most days.

When our nurturing "cup" is empty, it's time to refill it. We'll be happier and refreshed, and we'll have more positive attention to give to our children.

Also, they just might enjoy having "time off" from *you.*

DON'T:

DO:

Check out assumptions. Nobody is a mindreader. Many misunderstandings will be avoided.

We shouldn't assume that we know what's on another person's mind. "Innocent" assumptions can lead to misunderstandings or even major arguments.

If you were truly a mindreader, always 100% right, you would be on television, rich and famous, and you probably wouldn't be reading this advice book right now!

DON'T:

Rebecca won't mind if you take this sweater for your Stephanie. She never wears it.

Oh, thanks!

Uh-oh…

DO:

Rebecca, can Aunt Suzie take your sweater for Stephanie?

But it'll match this new skirt I just got!

Oh! Okay, never mind!

Check out predictions. Nobody can tell the future. You're showing respect by consulting the child first.

Predictions: same as assumptions. Some predictions can also become self-fulfilling prophecies, to the child's detriment. If we make negative predictions about our children, they will often prove us right by making them come true.

Samples:

- You're going to lose it.
- He's going to fail.
- She's not going to like it.

Better to be positive, and hope for the best instead!

DON'T:

DO:

Talk to your ex directly. You avoid putting your child in the confusing position of go-between.

Children shouldn't be used as messengers or "spies." This can be particularly harmful if we are in a constant state of war with our ex. It's like putting a child in the middle of crossfire in a battlefield; the child gets hurt by the verbal "bullets" the adults zing at each other.

Also, when we talk directly to each other, it helps unite the adults in the family as a parenting team. This is very important for our children's healthy psychological development.

DON'T:

DO:

Talk about your ex in a way that doesn't put her/him down. You make your ex *and* yourself look good. Your child is the winner!

Whenever we denigrate our ex, two harmful things happen:

We set up a loyalty conflict in our child. He/she becomes very torn between which parent is "right," which parent deserves to be loved more, which parent should be defended or blamed, and so on.

We damage your child's image of the other parent. Do we really want *our* anger and *our* hurt to affect our kids this way?

If our ex is truly a bad person, our child will discover it soon enough without our help!

Meanwhile, we must remember we're both on the same side: we both want the best for our children.

DON'T:

DO:

Present a united front. As a team using compromise, you'll impress your child with your solidarity and fairness. Neither parent will be stuck in the role of the "heavy" or the "pushover."

Parents should try to get together on discipline issues. It's best to consult each other privately when working out a consequence for misbehaviour or a limit to be set in advance. If we don't do this, we will have a "good cop/ bad cop" set-up, and the kids will have a great time bouncing each parent against the other.

DON'T:

DO:

Be cool: try not to argue with your ex in front of the kids. Keeping your talks private will target your feelings where they belong – not on your children.

Usually, "cool" parents = "cool" kids. The exception to this occurs when parents bottle up all their anger. This leads to tension, resentment and irritability with the children over minor issues – things we wouldn't normally care that much about, if we weren't so darn upset. Our angry and hurt feelings meant for our ex-spouse must go *somewhere*.

If direct discussion with our ex is impossible, talk to another adult – counsellor, friend, relative – in private. Ask someone to mediate, if necessary. We'll feel better, and so will our kids.

DON'T:

DO:

RESPECT – PART I – PROPERTY
Respect every family member's belongings.

In my experience as a family support worker, I found that **mutual respect** is a must. There are three main types of respect that we all deserve:

I – PROPERTY: SPACE FOR OUR STUFF
II – PHYSICAL: SPACE FOR PRIVACY
III – PSYCHOLOGICAL: SPACE TO THINK

Notice they're all about "space." The common denominator regarding spaces is that each space has **boundaries**. In families we need to learn to respect each other's boundaries.

Generally when we give people respect, they give it back to us.

~~~

I – PROPERTY

When we respect each other's **property**, we are saying: Your possessions belong to you, I value you, and I value your possessions.

Neither adults nor kids like having their belongings mishandled or taken by someone else. Asking permission always helps.

DON'T:

DO:

RESPECT – PART II – PHYSICAL
Respect every family member's right to privacy.

II – PHYSICAL

Respect for each other's **privacy** leads to feelings of increased self-worth… and fewer arguments.

"Knock first!" A simple rule. When brothers or sisters share a bedroom, they should ideally each be allotted a definite area with clearly marked boundaries.

The logic is: we all deserve our own physical space. Others must ask if they may enter it; this shows respect for us.

The need for privacy increases with the age of the child, and certainly includes parents too!

DON'T:

DO:

RESPECT – PART III – PSYCHOLOGICAL
Respect your child: spare her your adult concerns.

III - PSYCHOLOGICAL

We have to respect our child's status as our offspring – she or he is not our best friend or therapist.

We need to avoid drawing our kids into details beyond their concern. Whether our child is five or twenty-five, he or she should not be our confidante.

If we're a single parent, as in the example shown, our unique issues can be discussed with a good friend, relative, co-worker, or therapist – *not* with our children. Our kids have their own troubles. It's our job to help *them*, not vice-versa.

If we're married, there also may be times that we're tempted to unload our feelings, worries etc. on our kids. Often it's the eldest one who serves as the inappropriate sounding board. Yes, yes, they're there, they're so *handy,* after all. And sometimes they're *such good listeners*. But Mom? Dad? Don't. Just don't. It's not their role.

5. Summary

So just to sum up – some nice "A" words to shoot for in your family would include:

- Appreciation (so prized)
- Affection (always enjoyed!)
- Acceptance (better than rejection!)
- Attention (given positively!)

And some "C" words:

- Consideration
- Courtesy
- Cindness – oops, I mean, Kindness (This alliteration thing is harder than it looks!)

But above all:

Simply treat others the way you would like to be treated. It's known as – and I may have mentioned it before –

R E S P E C T

ACKNOWLEDGEMENTS

I owe many thanks to Shane Simmons and John Boone for their help in proofreading, formatting and beta-reading this book.

ABOUT THE AUTHOR

Ellie Presner worked as a social counsellor in Montreal during the 1980s. At the Parent Enrichment Project she specialized in teaching parenting skills, and later at Ville Marie Social Service Centre she was a family-support worker helping families in difficulty.

Ellie taught "Introduction to Intervention with Families" at Dawson College's Social Service Department.

Ellie and her two children managed to survive in a single-parent household.

SPECIAL THANK YOU

Last but definitely not least, thanks so much to my children, Kathryn and Jeremy, for letting me practise on them for a couple of decades.

www.ingramcontent.com/pod-product-compliance
Lightning Source LLC
Chambersburg PA
CBHW060146050426
42448CB00010B/2315